The Haiku Aesthetic:

Short Form Poetry

as a Study in Craft

Jean LeBlanc

For George Lightcap,

whose classroom is never without haiku

Acknowledgments

"Two Or So Brushstrokes" appeared in *Off-Line: An Anthology of New Jersey Poets*, South Mountain-Watchung Poets, Inc., 2010.

"Teaching Tanka," parts 1 and 2, were originally published in *Modern English Tanka* no. 4, Summer, 2007, the tanka journal of MET Press. This article was then reprinted in the MET Press publication *Tanka Teachers Guide*, 2007. A special thanks to editor Denis M. Garrison for all his work at MET Press over the years.

The online journal *tinywords* (http://tinywords.com) first published "white phlox blossoms..." (issue 11.1); "gleam of cattails..." (issue 11.1); "a crossword puzzle..." (issue 11.2); "a new path..." (issue 11.2); "thunder..." (issue 11.3); "reminding myself..." (issue 13.1).

My essay on Judith A. Christian's haiku "rising from your bed" first appeared on the Haiku Foundation Blog *troutswirl*, in February of 2012, now archived at http://www.thehaikufoundation.org/2010/02/21/viral-6-4/. Thanks to Judith A. Christian and The Haiku Foundation (www.thehaikufoundation.org) for permission to reprint this essay.

Chuck Tripi's poem "State Street to Central, by Lark" was first published in *The Stillwater Review*, Issue #2 (2012); this poem also appears in his collection *Carlo and Sophia* (Cyberwit.net, 2013).

Jim Berkheiser's poem "Hidden Treasure" first appeared in *The Stillwater Review*, Issue #1 (2011).

Introduction

In October of 2011, I facilitated a writing workshop called The Haiku Aesthetic. We filled a classroom at Sussex County Community College on a gray Saturday morning as the first few flakes of an unusual autumn blizzard began to fall. I look back at that morning as one of the highlights of my poetry life. The room was a warm, laughter-filled island oblivious to the cold and threatening weather. This setting, in fact, seems to me in retrospect a perfect example of the paradox inherent in haiku, one of the elements of the haiku aesthetic I shared that day in the workshop.

I hope I convinced the workshop participants that the haiku aesthetic can be an element of all their poems, whether haiku, tanka, or longer poems. One of the points I tried to make was that the question, "Is it a good poem?" should precede even, "Is it a good haiku?" Each of these creations we poets write is, foremost, a poem, and must succeed as such; only then can we say, "And, it's a haiku" or sonnet or villanelle or unrhymed poem with twenty lines of varying length. The haiku aesthetic is the aesthetic of each poem, whatever its form.

I have been thinking about this every day since that workshop, wishing I could take the inspiration I felt in that room full of wonderful people and re-animate it in the pages of a book. It is, however, daunting to contemplate writing a book about haiku, since so many fine books about haiku already exist. I have decided, therefore, to approach the topic in a way that is personal rather than scholarly. I cannot claim—nor do I want to claim—that I am an expert on haiku. I am a poet who considers herself a life-long student of poetry, and that is the experience I want to try to share in the following pages: my own journey (so far) with haiku and related forms, as well as how I endeavor to infuse all my work with the haiku aesthetic.

By "the haiku aesthetic," I mean any paradox that makes a poem seem to come to life, suddenly more than a sprinkling of words. It is what translates that sprinkling of words into a little holding of breath by the reader, or a little "oh!" from the reader's lips. In preparing for my workshop on this topic, I studied my favorite haiku and listed the paradoxical qualities I saw in them. Almost all had a surface simplicity that gradually revealed a deeper complexity. Some of the haiku were austere in their simplicity, yet they had an elegance that felt almost monumental. Many had a melancholy tone, yet also celebrated the beauty of the moment—a beauty that would pass, or was in the process of passing. These haiku each in some way achieved balance, yet in some way also felt as if about to tumble off the page. Each had materiality—physical presence in the real world, anchored by strong images—but also ethereality, a delicateness that seemed too fine for this world. In each, something was said, but more was unsaid. To say that last another way: In a well-crafted haiku, something is said, but more—sometimes much more—is understood. To say *that* another way: In a well-crafted *poem*, something is said, but more—sometimes much more—is understood.

These paradoxical qualities are found in the most well-crafted, meaningful, beautiful poems, poems in which the poet exercised deliberation, discretion, and precision of expression. In this book, I would like to share my journey with haiku, tanka, and haibun, and also show how engaging in the practice of these forms can benefit all poets.

Part One: Haiku

wasn't I just here—
a yellowflag iris
catching the sun

thin silver bracelets
a hundred of them
if I had her arms

pure oxygen
her hand for a moment
so blue

geode bookends—
with a good swing, a student
could crack my skull

frayed cuffs is there a sky tonight

deep in thought
a granite woman
with a stone bouquet

the pear
and the white lilac
blooming as one

white bird
the lake is dark enough
without you

for you, sparrows,
the tall lilies
covered with aphids

if this were all
I knew, the meadow
at dawn

white phlox blossoms daring the frost

a crossword puzzle
side by side my parents

gleam of cattails and a high half moon

a new path—
little bones
around the fox's den

thunder
at the bus stop
the posture of rain

across my arm
where I walked too close
to the rose

old man
don't blame your dog for wanting
to go home

the path
not so much a path
as a place to stand

watching a boy I don't know
get your exact haircut
kingfisher

all tulip shapes the midnight garden

music
from a classroom
not mine

in the kitchen
the soft assent of something
touching something

his profile
as he packs for a trip
poem by poem

all these years
still looking for your footprints
in the soft red earth

porch after porch
the evening song of robins
roses after rain

what does it want
the constant whine
of Route 80

solstice moon
learning the names
of all these flowers

hummingbird
the almost-comfort
of present tense

the final night
this mountain will spy
on my dreams

dragonfly eyes—
turquoise in these hills
copper in those

Two Or So Brushstrokes

The pearl earring—two
brushstrokes, one expert avers.
I don't believe it.

But do we call it
Girl in Turban?—of course not.
It's those two brushstrokes.

Or her eyes: hazel?
Blue? Brown? Who can remember?
Shadows, highlights, both

or light and not light,
two or so, our expert says—
a dab doesn't count?

If I could paint you
what would my two brushstrokes be?
Cheekbone. Clavicle.

This is how to live—
keep what you love most
two or so brushstrokes away.

Writing and Revising Haiku

In his journal, the 19th-century American essayist, poet, and Transcendentalist philosopher Ralph Waldo Emerson wrote, "The art of writing consists in putting two things together that are unlike and that belong together like a horse and cart. Then have we somewhat far more goodly and efficient than either." He was certainly not specifically referencing haiku in that journal entry, but one can imagine that he was by that perfect evocation of the perfect haiku: "putting two things together that are unlike and that belong together."

And I like that he did not use "but"—he didn't say, "that are unlike *but* that belong together." He used "and." This evokes something even more basic about the haiku aesthetic: the feeling that the paradox is natural and unforced. As a poet, I know this moment when a poem I am writing turns into a discovery I am making. The words on the page suddenly make me feel I have seen something new because of them, even though I'm the one who put those words there. For that moment, however, it feels as if the words put themselves there. This feeling does not happen often, but when it does my first thought (after that initial wordless moment of communion with the words on the page) is, *Good, the poem is finished; no more revising.*

I have heard some poets say they love the revision process. I am not one of them. And haiku, I have found, require the most revision of any of the poems I write. The shorter the poem, the more prominent each word of the poem is, the more importance each word of the poem carries. The shorter the poem, the more crucial each line becomes. The shorter the poem, the more psychological consequence each line break needs to deliver. Only two line breaks in a three-line haiku: each line break must make total sense, marring neither the grace nor the flow of the poem, but contributing to the layers of meaning that the reader will realize in the two or three seconds it takes to read the haiku. Looking back at what I have written in this paragraph, I begin to believe it is simply impossible to write a haiku at all.

For me, the idea for a haiku begins with an image; the image, in turn, usually contributes to a line or two. *Five or six sparrows*, I said to myself one recent frosty morning, seeing the small brownish birds in the undergrowth, each flitting about so quickly I couldn't count them accurately. *There is something to that*, I began to think, something to not being able to know for certain, even with such a small thing—a small number, a small creature, a small moment. Just today, observing a January thaw in action here in the Northeastern United States: *a south-facing hillside, no snow lingers*. The different types of waves and ripples caused by the wind on different parts of the lake—I haven't been able to craft that image into any semblance of a haiku-worthy line or two or three. But these images are in my mind and in my notebook, and one day...

So I have notebooks full of images:

leaving school escorted by dragonflies

somewhere in the world
an eclipse

from grave to grave
with ebony wings

gravel road
a walker's every step

collecting stories about fireflies
the ringing in my right ear

I was not able to go on and grow a haiku from these images. Sometimes, the image itself seems like two-thirds of a haiku already— but there is only poem or no poem, there are no fractions of poems. I have the horse, but not the cart, as Emerson might say. No, that's not quite accurate: one could go somewhere with the horse alone. Those images are the cart, but there is nothing to make the cart *go*. The images just sit there, immobile, decorative but useless, without context. It is my biggest challenge, avoiding calling a poem a haiku that is *merely* an image. It is a cliché, of course, the writing teacher's old saying. "Show, don't tell." That is sometimes modified into "too much tell." Well, there is also such as thing as "too much show," and to my mind, an image without context is an image without meaning.

To me, a successful haiku—even one whose subject is stillness and contemplation—feels as if it is about to tumble off the page. I feel somehow askew when reading the poem. Balance and surprise: this is an important paradox in the haiku aesthetic. Even when I can go beyond the decorative image and approach something haiku-like, I often fail to achieve a poem that will "spring balance" onto the reader, or surprise the reader with an unlikely poise.

> high ground
> from which to see
> the sun

> the stream
> so small you would
> never think

They just do not contain anything that surprises me, those two failed haiku. There is no "ah ha!" moment. As my own toughest critic, I admit those haiku have more of a "So what?" moment. Thus, they remain in my notebook, or here in this paragraph about failed haiku.

Sometimes a failed haiku keeps calling to me, such as one I tried to capture after walking in my favorite place a couple weeks after a hurricane damaged many trees. I wanted to describe what I saw, the paradox of usefulness even amidst destruction...

>   so many trees down
>   an unexpected bounty
>   for the porcupines

...but it just doesn't come alive on the page. I think it's that word "capture." I hear that word used often when people discuss this form, how a haiku "captures" a moment. That doesn't seem quite accurate to me. There is no "capturing" time. Part of the power of a haiku is that the moment feels all the more beautiful for having slipped away—fuller, more realized, gone. A haiku sets aside a moment for a moment in the normal course of things to be a little more appreciated. A haiku is retrospection in the present tense. When I sit down to write with the idea of "capturing" anything, especially time, the result is disappointing, usually not a poem I want to show to the world.

When I can incorporate an image plus some sense of balanced surprise into a haiku, there are still uncertainties that lead to revision. Here are several revisions of the same haiku (though they aren't the same):

>   this road—
>   the blur of autumn colors
>   all year long

>   this road a blur
>   of autumn colors
>   all year long

>   a blur, this road—
>   autumn colors
>   all year long

I seem to prefer "all year long" as the third line, though I could also try:

> all year long
> this road a blur
> of autumn

I like that one, because without the word "colors" the word "autumn" is free to evoke more than just the standard visual image of the changing foliage. In this case, revising has made me see deeper into my own poem, allowing me to re-vision the possible layers of meaning. This is revision at its best; this is the aspect of revision that meets with the blankest of blank stares as I try to convince my first-year college students to re-vision their essay first drafts.

An image, yes, but something more. Some sense of motion (even a motion of the mind), or some sort of surprise (though that is a dangerous word, for the surprise must be subtle—the paradox must reside just below the surface). A precarious balance. These are some of my ways of articulating the qualities of a successful haiku.

Part Two : Tanka

random words—
what I love about
old notebooks—
    corydalis
        meadow rue

to make conversation
he asks questions
that have no answers—
tire tracks
in a fallow field

for new guests
I describe
every nighttime noise
the house
will make

reading her letter
from last autumn—
through tall grass
a line of deer
in winter dun

an entire season
in this spot—
from no dragonflies
to dragonflies
to none again

on the headstone
1837–
no one remains
to tell the stonecarver
carve

back then
you could probably see
the river from here—
a falling away
of green into green

reminding myself
this isn't the first sunrise
she didn't see—
just the first we saw
without her

the November marsh—
memories
of memories, really—
the weight of sunlight
on broken reeds

imagining
how it would look,
this garden—
a strong back
and two good knees

a new way down
to the water's edge—
a dip
of earth
between boulders

driving
from pond to pond
looking for geese—
all that homework
waiting on my desk

the time of day
I love most
on campus—
more owls
than students

putting myself
in that alternate world
he says—
have I given him
my wine glass by mistake

his heart broken
by a foolish girl—
even I'm surprised
how much I can see
from this window

let's agree, you and I,
to go through life with no shame—
by August
the pond is choked
with lilies

the sequence we hope
to remember:
her face in pain
her face in moments of rest
her face as she sings and sings

the note you left me
folded like a flower
the handwriting
a swarm
of angry bees

winter afternoon—
talking about poets
and their funny ways,
why some birds migrate,
why some don't

winter's way
to try to woo us,
revealing
the hidden hillside
through the trees

the meadow
burned to stubble
not even wishing
I'd asked
for one more spring

do not put water
on to boil and then think,
I'll just run upstairs
to get
my glasses...

wishing for rain
the futility
of *serves you right*
and
told you so

back and forth
across the sky, a flock
of little ducks—
the third time today
I walk this trail

her low voice
in his bad ear—
somehow roses thrive
in this hot
dry land

sun on the mountaintop
late into the night
she keeps writing
knowing
it won't be for much longer

I am fine
until he asks me
to read her poem
that ends with the word
cold

morning
facing the wrong way
each story
turns to how
her mind—

he asks
about birds
but I am new here
even my own name
unfamiliar

losing track
of the days spent
in the desert
counting the age spots
on the back of my hand

His Hand in the River Changes the River

—for Peter Newton

the meadow suite
a little room filled
with robin song

a different bird and flower
on every page

with the spruce gone
seeing the four spruce trees
for the first time

cedar waxwings
in the honeysuckle—

is he that lonely
I think—but it's not bourbon,
it's maple syrup

his hand
in the river
changes
the river
changing me

Writing and Revising Tanka

After a few days of reading and writing haiku, a tanka suddenly seems epic. Narrative has five entire lines in which to leisurely unfold— a story with beginning, middle, and end almost seems possible! And the luxury of figurative language. "The note you left me / folded like a flower"—a simile! "Could it be / how winter tries to woo us"— personification! The danger is too much freedom—trying to do too much with the freedom of five lines.

If I think of an individual tanka as a story, I must also remember that the important part of the story is implied. It will be provided by an astute reader, and fifty astute readers will infer fifty important stories of their own. It is daunting and freeing at the same time. It allows me to think of each line of the tanka as a clue to the story, a little note to each reader that says "this way, this way, follow me." In addition, a paradox akin to that in a haiku gives the tanka added interest and provides an implied metaphor or even allegory. Follow me, but find your own path.

It also helps me to think of a tanka as a verbal photograph. A small photo, perhaps black and white, askew in a fading album in the back of a closet. Again, it is all about clues, each line a hint, not all the hints quite adding up. I often recall one favorite photograph, somehow a survivor of my family's penchant for throwing things away: the photographer was perhaps sitting down, because the figure of my grandmother looms in the middle distance, caught in mid-stride, walking into the wind, which shows in the wildness of her dark coat and hair. It was one of many too-early-in-the-season daytrips to the ocean, cold, windy, sandy picnics endured by people insistent that this was a good time, whether they were actually having a good time or not. My grandmother seems to me Shakespearian in this photo, more of a force than wind or sea, dominant, fierce, yet also lost. Lost to time, lost to the moment. And yet, here she is.

That is what I try to evoke in my tanka: something lost to time, lost even to its own moment, yet here it is, with me always. I approach every poem I write as a way of exploring something that intrigues or troubles me or holds my imagination in thrall; a tanka is no different, and should contain the same depth as a poem of twelve, fourteen, thirty lines. They don't all work, my tanka. Some veer a little too far off into the philosophical:

> same gray sky
> same low clouds
> would I be lying
> if I called this
> a journey

To me, that poem sounds flat, hampered by its own grayness and cliché. But that's fine; every exploration leads to a few places where one must retrace some steps in order to find a new route. Every poem is a learning experience, and I find it instructive to examine a poem that falls flat and see what makes it thus. "Same gray sky" does one thing I try to avoid in a tanka: it has two consecutive lines which, when isolated, provide no image: "would I be lying / if I call this." The word "lying" is almost strong enough to be a psuedo-image, but no, it falls short.

There is also no sense of motion in "Same gray sky"—not a fatal flaw in and of itself, but add that to the "dead space" of two image-free lines, and there's a poem that does not lift off the page to greet the reader with news of what is in that reader's heart. Earlier, I spoke of the lines of a tanka as hints, with not all the hints quite adding up. The paradox is that the hints don't quite add up, and yet they add up to something more. "Suggest" is perhaps a better word than the phrase "add up." "Same gray sky" lacks this "something more."

In notebooks, I may work and rework lines, playing with words that connote those elusive hints. A notebook page may look something like this:

same gray sky	yesterday's gray sky
same low clouds	and low clouds
would I be lying	this journey
if I called this	more like standing still
a journey	

yesterday's gray sky	yesterday's gray sky
and low clouds	this journey
you will say I'm lying	more like standing still

a journey
to yesterday's gray sky

And that notebook page may turn into two pages if I keep working at the idea, image, and lines. Line breaks are another aspect of poetry that I give a lot of attention to in my haiku and tanka. The difference between "yesterday's gray sky / this journey / more like standing still" and "yesterday's gray sky / this journey more like / standing still" is subtle, but I don't like ending a line on a non-image or non-verb ("this journey more like"). It goes back to crafting each line into that little hint, and while there is something intriguing about hearing only "this journey more like," to my ear (and eye, when on the page) it feels unsatisfying.

As a way of critiquing my line breaks in a tanka, I look at the last words of each line and see if they alone provide the hints to the narrative. My next-to-the-last draft of one of my tanka was this:

> he asks me
> about the birds I saw
> but I am new here
> even my own name
> unfamiliar

Using the last-word-of-each-line technique results in "me saw here name unfamiliar"—not especially compelling words on which to end the first four lines. This led me to realize I don't need to be so verbose, that I can hone the lines down to this:

> he asks
> about birds
> but I am new here
> even my own name
> unfamiliar

That feels more concise, more trusting of the reader to understand that "he" was asking "me" about what "I saw." And it results in the last word of each line sequence being "asks birds here name unfamiliar," the images a bit more interesting. The word at the end of line will have a fraction of a second longer to linger in a reader's consciousness as that reader's eyes travel to the beginning of the next line. I think of this as I craft my line breaks in every poem I write, hoping to "leave" the reader with an image or feeling that is worthy of that extra resonance.

Having spoken of how I found I could "hone the lines" to make that tanka more "concise," I want to emphasize here that I do *not* consider "minimalism" an element of the haiku aesthetic. Precision of language and presentation of the image in a focused, concentrated verbal frame does not mean simply "paring" the language down into a clipped, unnatural syntax. A poem of three, five, or any number of lines should feel lush—the poem should be a portal into a new way of seeing, perhaps into a new world. I avoid references to "minimal" when I discuss haiku and tanka, while still encouraging a close look at language and how best to articulate image and thereby suggest meaning(s).

In my chapter on writing and revising haiku, I spoke of some images being "too much show" and not enough meaning. I have experienced this in tanka, as well. The final tanka I deleted from this manuscript was this one:

> from every canyon
> a hundred side canyons—
> in each story
> the beginning
> of several more

I thought that was a perfect tanka, and clung to it through several drafts of this manuscript. I finally had to admit, however, that it is too simile-like; a canyon is like a story.... While a tanka can contain figurative language, this one was just too obvious, maybe even tending toward cliché. That image of a hundred side canyons haunts me, but I predict I'll never successfully incorporate it into a tanka.

With each poem I write, I am surprised by how the elements of craft work together toward the success or failure of the work. A faulty line break can obscure meaning. The perfect line break can add layers of meaning, for in the millisecond it takes for the reader's eyes to move to the beginning of the next line, suggestions will have awakened into possibilities. An image lacking subtlety makes for a clunker of a poem— the precarious balance of the haiku aesthetic is lost. Always the haiku aesthetic leads me to consider each tanka with the scrutiny I would bring to a longer poem: Does the poem offer, with each reading, a paradox waiting to be rediscovered? Is each line is a hint of what's to come? Is each line a hint of what was?

Teaching Tanka
Part 1: Challenges and Rewards

The first thing I notice when I'm introducing tanka to a writing class is: I would like to have a dollar for every time I use the oxymoron "deceptively simple." This applies to the tanka themselves, and, as I learned in the classroom, it also applies to the practice of teaching students to write this lovely and venerable form.

My first mistake seemed a logical first step: defining "tanka." For this, I showed my students the definitions on the website for the Tanka Society of America. I read aloud how a tanka is an "often lyrical, chiefly five-line poem" (TSA "What is Tanka" site) with a "subtle turn" (Pat Shelley, qtd. in "What is Tanka?") that "takes us from the simple to the complex (Gerald St. Maur, ibid.).

Immediately, my students' faces betrayed their thoughts: a five-line poem that needs all these abstract, philosophical, ambiguous definitions, each one slightly different from the next? I had made them defensive against something that I wanted them to enjoy. I compounded this problem by explaining the 5-7-5-7-7 traditional syllable count, while in the same breath encouraging them to ignore this and concentrate on writing five short-ish lines.

I should mention that my class is made up of students working toward their degrees in English with teaching certification. Besides taking literature and education courses, these students are juggling student teaching, praxis exams, and the daily red tape inherent in any specialized course of study. Their minds are fine-tuned to the letter of the myriad rules, regulations, and deadlines that will allow them to graduate and become certified teachers. I should never have thrown that 5-7-5-7-7 "rule" at them; that stuck, and for a little while, creativity suffered.

My second (or third—I'm already losing count) mistake was teaching tanka right after we did haiku. While many definitions allude to the kinship of tanka and haiku, you might as well say a spider is akin to a lobster. It's true, but what does that tell us about the nature of either spiders or lobsters? Heck, aside from cultural origin, a tanka is akin to a sonnet, in that they both use descriptive and metaphorical language, they both contain a turn from observational to philosophical, and they're both poems. Haiku was successful in getting my students to focus the outward world, but it was difficult for them to then effect that inward turn that tanka requires. "Leave yourself out of the haiku," I said. "Put yourself in the tanka," I said. They ended up disliking both forms in this game of poetic Simon Says.

But perhaps I am wrong to use the word "mistake" in describing my tanka teaching experiences. There's no such thing, after all, as a failed experiment. When I handed back their first round of tanka, my students all asked for a chance to further revise their work. I knew I had to help them find a "new way in" to their understanding of the tanka form.

The next time I teach a lesson on writing tanka, I'll start by showing examples. Or better yet, reading examples. I'll have the students listen and then write their thoughts as I read a tanka to them a few times. I think the hypnotic quality of a perfectly-formed tanka will set their imaginations free. Try this for yourself: have a friend choose a tanka from the pages of *MET* or *Ribbons* or another tanka journal, and while you sit and listen, have your friend read that one poem to you three times. You see something new in each reading; the same words stimulate new associations; the images form and re-form. Meaning emerges. Ambiguity evolves into layers of clarity.

I found another way to re-introduce my students to tanka. This sounds counter-intuitive, but I moved us to a room with computers. This room has a "smart board," onto which is projected whatever is shown on the teacher's computer screen. I could call up the website for *Modern English Tanka* and have hundreds of examples for the class to see. Furthermore, each student could log on to the site and find tanka that spoke to them. Much better than the page or two of examples I could show them the "old-fashioned" way, by photocopying handouts.

A good teacher is always open to the one thing you can't write into a lesson plan: serendipity. Along came the Spring, 2007 issue of *Ribbons*, and there was an elegant, insightful article by Jeanne Emrich titled, "A Quick Start Guide to Writing Tanka." This article, coupled with Emrich's earlier article "A Tanka Repair Kit," provided our in-class breakthrough. Emrich highlighted the technique of making the tanka's third line its "pivot line." This helped my students see what I meant by what I called the "tanka twist."

Using *Ribbons* and *MET*, I had my students find examples of tanka that exhibit the third-line-pivot, and tanka that use a different technique to effect that inward-looking twist. We compared two tanka by the same poet, Chuck Tripi. His tanka in the Spring, 2007 *Ribbons*,

> a posture of mine,
> sleep—invisible, yielding
> midnight and I
> carefully peering
> all the way into you

has that third line that can go with either the first two or the last two lines. One of Chuck Tripi's tanka in the Spring, 2007 *MET*, however, does not have this central pivot line:

> You are dancing in the other room,
> two steps and a circle, you smile.
> Who is he,
> the gentleman
> not there with you?

Here the "twist" comes from the unexpected "not" in the fifth line, and all its implications of secrets, jealousy, desire. At last, with Emrich's articles and a bounty of published tanka for inspiration, my students were more at ease with this deceptively simple form.

I asked each student to write the first two lines of a tanka, the simple, outward observation, the image. (I made this two lines, not three, so as not to raise the specter of haiku). As they were writing two or three two-line observations, I chose three lines from a published tanka. I wrote the students' two lines on the board and "finished" each with the inward-looking "emotion" or "experience" of the three lines I had chosen at random (same three lines for each student). It was an epiphany, to see how these hybrid tanka offered insight and often delightful juxtapositions of image/experience.

"Not many tanka use that 5-7-5-7-7 syllable count," one of my students said as she perused the on-line pages of *MET*.

I knew they were ready to make their way into this deceptively-simple form.

References:

Emrich, Jeanne. "A Quick Start Guide to Writing Tanka." *Ribbons, Tanka Society of America Journal.* 3(1): Spring 2007. 25. (This article originally appeared in "The Critical Poet," <http://www.criticalpoet.com>, and also appears at <www.tankaonline.com>.)

——. "A Tanka Repair Kit." *Ribbons, Tanka Society of America Journal.* 2(1): Spring, 2006. 13.

Tanka Society of America. Home page <http://www.tankasocietyofamerica.com> and "What is Tanka?" link, <http://www.tankasocietyofamerica.com/Tankadefined.hym>. Site as visited on 15 April 2007 for preparation of this article.

Tripi, Chuck. Tanka, "You are dancing." *Modern English Tanka*, 1(3): Spring 2007. 156.

——. Tanka, "a posture of mine." *Ribbons, Tanka Society of America Journal.* 3(1): Spring 2007. 21.

Part 2: Vision and Revision

In front of me now, I have several pages of my students' notebooks, which illustrate the challenge of the revision process for the tanka form.

My first step was to help them recognize and eliminate repetition. Almost simultaneously, step two was to encourage them to pare down the imagery; their tanka were often overflowing with images, leaving little room for inward reflection. Chrissy Vnencak wrote this first draft:

> Dangling from my neck
>
> an emerald stone sways
>
> on a chain
>
> as I walk
>
> the only object Grandma left me

This tanka contains three images of motion: dangling, swaying, and walking; three visual images: a woman's neck, the green pendant, the chain; and then, after these six strong images all vying for dominance, the tanka attempts to look inward at the legacy of love.

A much-scribbled over second draft shows proposed and rejected lines about "another day of stress" and "its old owner." Eventually Chrissy showed me a third draft, in which she had changed lines four and five to:

> Its smoothness against my chest is comfort,
>
> The only object my grandmother left me.

This draft had eliminated the image of walking—good, since the swaying pendant made the walking motion redundant—but added the tactile image of smoothness, as well as the in-scape of comfort. My creative writing students wrote stunning sonnets, villanelles, list poems, and longer free-verse poems—ah, the tanka form is a challenge unto itself! I was glad to see that at least they had been able to put aside the 5-7-5-7-7 format. Now, if I could just get them to "think short."

After another page of revisions, Chrissy's tanka came to be:

> Around my neck
>
> an emerald stone
>
> dangling on a chain.
>
> Grandma
>
> still able to comfort me.

Lovely, how the idea of legacy becomes implied, and comfort carries the day. I could have suggested to Chrissy that she change "dangling" to "dangles," and shorten the ending even more, to something along the lines of "Grandma/still comforts me." But like a longer poem, tanka can suffer from being "overworked" in the revision process, having all the life and singularity of voice stifled until the poem sounds like a bland, authorless product of yet another creative writing workshop. Better, I think, to let students discover their own idiom, their own way of bringing image and idea to life on the page.

With tanka, as with haiku, students seem to want to leave out small words such as articles and conjunctions, and sometimes forms of the verb "to be," giving the haiku or tanka a choppy, unnatural syntax. And, of course, there's the opposite tendency: wanting to turn the tanka into a narrative poem that shows and says way too much.

Another challenge in teaching tanka in a workshop setting is the aspect of time. A tanka should capture a moment, but there scarce seems to be such thing as a singular "moment" in the lives of my students. I begin class by reminding them that their portfolios are due in X number of weeks, and their group presentations are the week after that; I hear them discussing finals and other deadlines for their other classes...so how can I be surprised that their tanka, far from concentrating on "this moment," instead take on the aspect of mini-epics:

> Two years gone by
> Nothing but papers, deadlines.
> Graduation to come,
> The long anticipated day.
> Now I have to find a job.

That was a first draft by Beverly Wood, who also has young children; she began another tanka with the lines "Small yesterday / Grown today / A man tomorrow." Past, present, and future! That is the 'moment" in the busy lives of these English education majors. Beverly was able to capture the essence of a "strawberries and cream" experience in another tanka. This all served to remind me that an ephemeral sensory experience, plus deeper emotional associations, are often inimical to a classroom setting, where everything is ruled by the clock. A sobering lesson indeed for a creative writing instructor.

Of course, it speaks volumes for the form of the tanka itself, that students want to use it as a means of narrative. Distilling a story down to its essence—an image, an emotional response—is the intellectual exercise that makes tanka such a worthy challenge. There is so little in the routine and business of daily life that is elegant. I thank my students for allowing me to observe them on their journey into elegance that is tanka writing.

The "third line pivot" worked nicely for Nicole Mackesy in her tanka that describes the rain "falling heavily." I love the image in her third line of "splashing sideways," obviously referring to the rain in lines 1 and 2, but also to the body in the bed trying to flail down into the covers and hide from the world. For Jamie Meny, too, the third line pivot provides a wistful twist in her tanka "innocent butterfly." The juxtaposition of pronouns bespeaks of the importance of these little words in a short poem: "I admire its freedom/planning my escape." Jamie adds a twist to this twist by alluding to the ultimate "escape" in her last line. Meanwhile, Amy Feld used a subtle third-line pivot and came close to writing what may be my students' signature form—the tanka epic:

> laundry dishes
> never ending carpools
> cooking cleaning driving
> waiting for it all to end
> wouldn't change a thing

And that's a perfect example of how to recognize a good poetry-writing "rule." If the rule is flexible enough to allow, in fact encourage, variations, it should be embraced (everyone loves a rule that just begs to be broken). By seeing the pivot line so eloquently explained in Jeanne Emrich's article, my creative writing students were able to better understand the outward-to-inward turn a tanka needs to craft a five-line microcosm of life experience.

Part Three : Haibun

My Little Way North

Every road is narrow, even the interstate. One more time, this journey toward the familiar shapes on the horizon, the Green Mountains. Surrounded by Vermont, in a place where I can guess the time by the sun's position in the sky, I find my favorite path, greet the wood sorrel. Welcome, say the ghosts I have come to visit. But that is my imagination, heavy with the past, with what is lost. Even knowing it will happen, the moment of finding the wood sorrel is a surprise.

in the cool
that follows sunset
mist rises
or settles
or both at once

How When You Love Someone

you think they must have been born rich in a beautiful house full of light. Or else they grew up deep in the forest where the light is always green. How when you love someone, the waterlilies bloom close to shore, close enough to wade out to them and see into their center. Oh that lovely mouth, you think. Oh that lovely hand. I was born poor, but now, but now—

> every gesture
> an angle of elbows
> an egret in every lake

Memory

The kitchen of the hunting cabin is filled with women: my mother, my father's sisters and sisters-in-law, me. I am ten, perhaps. The men are outdoors, smoking. My aunts speak halting English, my mother and I speak no French. "Cup of tea, Lucy?" is one sentence they all know, loving the rhyme of it, the upward inflection at the end. They say it again and again, each time with more hilarity, a nonsense phrase in some third language, in some unknown place—Maine, Quebec, no map really says for sure, the dirt road in crossing and re-crossing the border. And yes, it may be that I am thinking this now, looking back, but I think I knew it even then: My mother is relaxed, actually enjoying the moment, more than a little grateful for this casual silliness, feeling accepted into this club. A visitor made to feel welcome, so welcome as to laugh.

> *we don't know what*
> the nurse tells me
> *but at times something*
> *makes her smile*
> *and smile*

The Drive Home

Sunset—a pale drama in the sky above Main Street, above the boarding house, above the Baptist Church, above the nursing home. The combination of the church and my recent reading of *Moby Dick* brings Jonah into my mind. Poor Jonah, the reek of fish—how many hours in there until he would begin to dissolve, his flesh going pasty? How many hours can each of us stand, in our own private whale?

once
dreaming of fresh air
a field so green

Her Portrait

—Bianca Sforza, attributed to Leonardo da Vinci

After her death, someone cut her portrait from the book in which it had been bound. A still-new husband's only comfort? A courtier with an eye toward fortune? A lady-in-waiting, missing her new mistress? Whoever did the job was unsteady with the knife, making a little slip of grief or impatience or loneliness. And how she died—we do not know. Only her portrait, a profile, the eyes not meeting ours, looking inward to the book's spine, no longer there.

too frail
for northern winters
the funny Latin
of these
northern priests

the fingerprint
of the artist—
chalk, Leonardo

why entomb her twice—
the ribbon holding
every hair in place

Owls

The voices of fishermen carrying over the water? A car radio at the distant boat ramp? It seems too early for these sounds, so what is it I am hearing here on the lake shore? *The sound of sense*, Robert Frost called it, when you can hear but not hear, not hear yet begin to understand the nature of what is being said. Is it just the buzzing in my ears, seeming to come from without this morning? Then I realize: Owl! I am hearing an owl—no, two owls, answering one another. *Who who who-who...who who who-who*. From somewhere in the woods behind me, just barely reaching the water's edge.

>   *here*
>   my grandmother would order,
>   or was it, *hear*

>   here
>   but not here, the first night
>   in a new room

>   owl
>   I say, stubbing
>   my toe in the dark

Silence

One winter, to Thoreau's chagrin, Walden Pond rang and groaned beneath the ice-cutters' blades. Great blocks of frozen Walden, a foot thick or more, were hauled away, with cart runners crunching, horse teams steaming up the air, men shouting back and forth. Thoreau tried to feign interest in the work, the specialized tools, but he couldn't quite abide. They soon moved on to other ponds, the men and their saws and picks. Henry tossed and turned all night, wakeful in the newer, deeper silence.

barberry—
what did I do
with the path

little diving ducks
the lake all shards
of light

two hunters
their arrows the color
of autumn

Where She Is Now

We can only guess. Outside the window of her room there are trees that no one would call a forest. Some birds. A corner of lawn. Where she is now might be far away from now. Does she ever sit on the edge of her bed and watch the blue jays, the common crows? Does she think, *A bird feeder there on that hillside would be perfect.* Where could the word "perfect" lead. *There's that little hill, and if the feeder were near the bottom, I could reach to fill it myself, mornings.*

even empty
she'd carry it if she could,
her purse

I guess it's mine now
the necklace my mother
doesn't need

small mostly colorless birds
the flock that never changes

Soliloquy

Oh to have done better, to have found a way through this and out the other side into the light of a day exactly like this day, stringing up the clothesline, kissing the back of your neck as you secure the laundry against the wind, three clothespins for every garment. To have found a way for this to be so, here, now, is what I should have done. Instead, in my dreams, you look at me with a look that lets me know I am not the person you thought I was, not a person at all worthy of your love.

> the rain forms
> a little path of pine cones
> down the gentle slope

Her Boy Looks Just Like Her

Her eyes, even with his bangs as long as he can grow them and still
see. Her neck, a neck longer than a boy might want. Her mouth, though
on him it is a mouth given neither to smiling nor to frowning, just a line,
a straight and even line. Her cheekbones. Cheekbones you can easily
imagine wet with tears.

what color eyes—
ice on the Delaware
late in winter

whether it melts
or breaks suddenly
it will take with it
a handful of battered
island trees

do you want to live
close enough to know
what a river can do

All That Remains

Stone steps down the steep bank. A few concrete slabs, level with the surface of the lake.

> *low over the lake*
> *the heron makes her way*
> *near, nearer*

After the ceremony in the Wawayanda Lodge, a little celebration here. The new Eagle Scouts dance with their mothers. Candles line the edge of the dock, a hundred flames become thousands when the breeze picks up. There is a string quartet—boys from the troop, who at moments become a little mesmerized by the lights in the water, and almost forget to play. They only know a few pieces, all waltzes, but no one notices as they play them over and over.

> *do you see, heron, that there are pearls*

The dancers freeze at one woman's sudden *Oh!* She has hooked her necklace with her ring. The beads bounce a few times, some landing in the water. A few droplets, not really a splash at all. So many pearls going so many ways.

> *to the bluegills the heron a heron-shaped*
> *cloud*

She shrugs, makes a little gesture. It's nothing. Keep dancing, Nothing matters tonight except tonight.

> *low over the lake*
> *the heron makes her way*
> *near, nearer, gone*

Stone steps down the steep bank. A few concrete slabs, level with the surface of the lake.

Three Haibun Inspired by the Anglo-Saxon Poem "Wulf and Eadwacer"

Bathing

The deer have made a path down to the lake, with only a bramble here or there to catch my sleeves. A few moments with no eyes on me, the men still sleeping off last night's drink, the sun barely above the trees. I am sorry when I startle a little flock of ducks. Is nothing to be at peace with nothing in this world, perhaps not even in the next? The deer path leads to a small place of sand, soft on the bottom of my feet, sprinkled with white shells. Empty, beautiful, the shells. The wind, when there is wind, blows in this direction, and with the lake waves come the sand and shells. But now the surface of the water is still, except when it accepts my body without question, something at peace with something, at last.

> lifting her wings
> to catch the wind like sails
> the lone swan

Her Dream

Your head upon someone's spear, or tossed back and forth between these overgrown children. And if they threw your severed head my way? What a choice: to let it fall at my feet, a little gore staining the hem of my dress forever, your beautiful face—or to catch it in my arms, my fingers in your hair one final time? Surely you have escaped, no longer hidden on that island, no longer surrounded by these war-deluded men. All night their long knives gleam. My cries startle the watchers, who swear at a stupid female unused to their good strong life.

> the rising sun
> makes of this path
> one long shadow, fox

Not from Hunger, I Grow Ill

I showed the women how to use wild grapes to stuff the pigeons, five to a spit, roasted over open flames. My hands turned black from seeding the fruit, but that only made them love me more. I almost said, "How he would have laughed at me," meaning you, but I caught myself in time, you not being my husband, and therefore without leave to laugh at anything I do. But I hear it all the time, your laughter, in the crackle of the flames, in the breaking of the small bones as we bind the birds for cooking, anything non-human that makes a sound—the iron-against-iron of the turning spit, the wind of course, and always, always, the rain.

long before sunrise
doves calling, calling—
even as a child
I could never sleep
this late

Capitol Reef National Park

After a hike through a narrow canyon, I step—boots and all—into the Fremont River. A stream, we would call this back east, where it would hold its course. Stream-like today, but there are signs all around of this river's real nature: dry washes left and right that braid through the canyons; smooth canyon walls that curve where the river says *curve*. This is water that gets wider and wider, wilder and wilder. But for today, it is a refreshing wade, a chance to see dragonflies in the desert, violet-green swallows swooping overhead, a breeze in the cottonwoods along the banks.

it's singular, "sky,"
even with all these
different clouds

Antelope Island, Great Salt Lake

—for Michal Onyon

She asks me, how would an artist paint this landscape, which seems so desolate on a grand scale but which reveals so many details if one looks closely? One could approach it in elemental terms—earth and water, sun and wind. There is the curve of the shoreline, great sweeping arcs of land and lake from hillside to hillside. But I am a poet; I only know small things, such as the sweet-scented herb that thrives in the hard-packed ground. It is daunting to try to imagine, getting onto canvas this place that is not easily taken in by any or all of the senses. Desolate, harsh, unforgiving—our words for a place distant, ancient, unaccommodating.

> her eyes that find
> these piecemeal things
> and see them whole

Visitors

She tells the story with such equanimity that I think this must have happened years and years ago, when she was new to this unforgiving landscape with its coyotes and rattlesnakes and mountain lions. Her beloved cat (she points to a soft and graceful portrait of her pet, "That's him,—I drew that")—"We think it was a great horned owl...." Her one remaining cat strides into the kitchen, seeking attention. "We think he saw it happen from in here," she says of this cat, and I realize the owl's meal was recent, a week or so ago...

one painting
reflected in another—
a nighthawk soars
beneath the lovers'
outstretched arms

Later in the evening, with the same calm demeanor, she tells us about the spot on her lungs—this was two years ago—test after test inconclusive, "different machines, different technicians all saying something different. I had to say, 'no more tests.'" But now she is ready to learn more, feels better for having made the appointment.

except it isn't
a painting of lovers
but a landscape—
two mountains, the gentle slope
of each to each

Life Here

The rooms are filled with sunlight, and yet feel dark. There is a great silence, overwhelmed by the sound of ceaseless wind. Beauty is everywhere, but so many faces stare blankly at the floor. Once, beauty and love found refuge here—beauty and love created this place—but now they are outcasts looking in. Everyone at home, yet everyone an outcast looking in.

a dry spring
the penstemon gone early
to seed—
his hands the color
of petrified wood

Always a New Way of Seeing

Kath gives me the art book—*Keep it, you should have it,* she insists—delighted at my reaction to the artist's style. Slightly askew. Connected, image to image, idea to idea, color to color. Original perspective, like Kath's portrait of Ray, his hands in his lap, his knees, his right foot, the floor. ("I've got those same shorts on now!" Ray says.) Her paintings show her fearless quest for beauty, allowing for serendipity. Causing a reaction. Letting the subject suggest a story—letting the viewer provide the story, although the viewer may be wrong. Everything different, but part of a plan.

> architecture
> he calls it,
> as if the sego lily
> were a temple
> to the wind

Writing and Revising Haibun

I turn to haibun when I feel that the versatility of this form will accommodate the image-intensive poem I am trying to write, a poem with qualities both narrative and descriptive. A haibun guides the reader into a moment in time. Reading (and writing) a haibun is like being able to step into a moment and look around. I think of haibun as a way to suggest stream-of-consciousness, but stream-of-consciousness crafted into poetic form, with the flexible boundaries of narrative plus the subconscious mind's leaps of logic / leaps of faith as image evokes image evokes image.

A haibun consists of at least one prose-like paragraph, followed by at least one haiku or tanka. The haiku or tanka may be directly (and obviously) linked to the paragraph, or—and this increases the depth of this form—the transition may "skip a few steps," allowing the connections to be made by the reader. Or, if not exactly "made," at least wondered at.

I call the paragraph "prose-*like*" because it is, after all, a poem. As with the other short forms, images are the *raison d'être* of a haibun, though certainly more overt (if brief) narrative is a pleasing possibility. The language will benefit from compactness and concision; as with every poem, word choice is crucial. Because so much is possible with haibun, conscious and careful deliberation, discretion, and expression will infuse the poem with energy, meaning, and possibility. The haiku aesthetic is vital to the prose-like paragraph, with precise language balancing that which is shown and that which is left unsaid.

I have found in my own writing of haibun that I revise best the day after I have written a first draft. My prose-like paragraph feels perfect at first, but the following morning I find I can pare the language down a little more. While not interrupting the narrative flow, I want the images to stand out. Of course, I am describing the element of balance here. A haibun is a lesson in how revision can confer balance to any work.

A haibun's balance also depends on the second element of this form: the haiku or tanka *denouement*. This element must be good enough to stand alone, yet still benefit from the set up of the prose-like paragraph. It must provide a sense of closure while still leaving enough openness for the reader to find layers of meaning and multiple connections. I remind myself with every haibun I write that the haiku must not repeat what has already been said. The haiku also must not evoke what has already been evoked. The haiku should be apart, while still being a part.

I find that I use haibun mainly for two types of narrative: interior monologue and historical recreation. In "Owls," I wanted to retrace my thoughts as I stood at the edge of my favorite lake in the darkness before a winter dawn, wondering what the strange almost-but-not-quite human sounds were that I was hearing. I remember how the realization of owls "dawned" on me, and within a moment or two the owls went silent as the eastern sky grew imperceptibly lighter. From the re-creation of my inner monologue followed the haiku on the idea of the words "hear" and "owl," as well as the act of hearing-but-not-quite hearing, an auditory plus visual darkness and dislocation. The haiku extend the stream-of-consciousness feel of the paragraph's interior monologue. What I also love about this haibun experience was that I was at the lake to take photographs, but had arrived far too early for there to be adequate light for this. So I stood there, creating this photograph-in-words instead.

In "Silence," I also worked with the idea of sound, this time to animate the human activity on a small pond in Concord, Massachusetts, *circa* 1845. I write many poems inspired by historical events and people; only recently have I realized the potential of haibun as a vehicle for these evocations of the past. It is, for me, that idea of stepping inside a moment and having the luxury of time—or the luxury of no pressing sense of time—to look around, explore, and allow the world of my imagination come to life on the page.

I took that one step further with "Three Haibun Inspired by the Anglo-Saxon Poem 'Wulf and Eadwacer.'" Here I added the elements of the persona poem, using first-person point of view to imagine the experience of the unnamed narrator of that mysterious poem. How far removed from my own life is hers, and yet, in some ways, not—a powerful poem such as "Wulf and Eadwacer" shows how connected human experience is over time and distance, joy to joy, grief to grief. The prose-like portion of the haibun form felt natural and comfortable; the haiku and tanka were my personal connection to the life of the poem (reflecting my direct observation of the world around me) as well as a way to evoke the song-like lament and mystery of the work that inspired me.

I will tell you how much I love the haibun form: I feel that this form, above all others, offers a freedom for creativity, a sense of infinite possibility. Writing a haibun, or reading one, makes me feel I could do anything, if only I would try. There's a power in this form that is quite profound. That power is commensurate to the subtlety of the prose-like portion of the poem. Revision, for me, is a way to enhance the subtlety. "Enhanced subtlety"—how's that for an oxymoron? Sometimes this can be as small as excising a word that detracts from the narrative flow. In "Visitors," I first wrote, "She tells the story with such equanimity that I think this must have happened years and years ago, perhaps when she was new to this unforgiving landscape." The "perhaps" in that opening sentence, I realized, was redundant. Dilution of language is not a welcome feature of any poem.

Along with this type of revision comes knowing when specific information needs to be added to make an image the focal point of the poem. When I invite the reader to step inside this moment, what do I want the reader to see, hear, smell, taste, touch? How do I want that reader to feel? How do I want to satisfy that reader's curiosity, rewarding curiosity with a sense of wonder? That leap from curiosity to wonder is inherent in the haibun form, as the prose gives way to the haiku or tanka. However, the leap from curiosity to wonder occurs in every successful poem, regardless of form; in a haibun, it's just reinforced by the obvious change on the page from prose-like paragraph to short-form poem. Furthermore, there is an implied trust in the change from prose-like paragraph to poem, a trust on the part of the reader that this short-form poem I'm about to experience is in some organic way connected to the prose-like paragraph that preceded it. Don't tell me how it's connected; let the connection(s) be the thing(s) that alchemize my curiosity into wonder. What leads us from moment to moment; what makes us look back on a moment and realize, long after the fact, that the moment was connected in a deeper way to what came before and/ or after? Why do *non sequiturs* sometimes make more sense than linear reality does? The psychology of memory and cognition is almost mapped out in haibun, displaying for us the inner workings of consciousness.

Be subtle, but be precise. Or, more accurately: Be precise, but be subtle. That is my note to myself as I write and revise haibun.

Part Four : The Haiku Aesthetic

In my American Literature II class recently, a student asked, "Do poets realize all the ways their work will be interpreted?" This is just one of the profound questions at the heart of all poetry, whatever the form—blank verse, free verse, sonnet, haiku. Form is a vehicle for meaning, after all; without meaning, form is an empty exercise. How did I answer that insightful question? I hope in this way: The better the poet, the more he/she realizes there will be as many meanings as there are readers. This is hyperbole, but it is an acknowledgment that a poem is not complete until it has a reader, a reader who brings additional meaning to the poem. No poem (or painting or dance) is the same poem (or painting or dance) twice. Once the poem leaves the poet's hands, it becomes new upon each reading.

Part of this is the haiku aesthetic at work. The newness of each rereading (even by the same reader), the freshness, the layers of insight, the increasing appreciation of the beauty of the work—all this energy, is what I think I mean when I speak of the haiku aesthetic. And all this energy doesn't just happen; this is the work of poetry, the craft, the conscious choices made by the poet that result in this new thing that the reader understands, having felt it before in a wordless way. A new thing that is immediately understood— another aspect, to my mind, of the haiku aesthetic.

When writing a poem, a poet turns his or her attention to certain elements of craft: imagery, line breaks, ambiguity balanced with clarity, diction (word choice) and syntax (word order), paradox, metaphorical meaning—all of these may be in the poet's consciousness as the poem progresses, or one or two may be uppermost on the poet's mind, but all these elements (and more) of craft must work together for a poem to come alive on the page and resonate with readers. All these elements of craft can be seen in this thing called "the haiku aesthetic," which was the link that got me thinking about using the study and practice of haiku, tanka, and haibun as a way to see anew one's longer poetic works. Let me offer a brief analysis of three poems that, to me, embody the haiku aesthetic.

*****

rising from your bed
remembering
the train whistle

—Judith A. Christian

I tell my students in Freshman Composition, "As with any poem, you can write a two- to three-page analysis of a well-crafted haiku." Their eyes grow wide with . . . terror? Disbelief? The excitement of a creative and intellectual challenge? Well, terror, then. That is what I feel now, as I try to find the words to describe everything I hear and see and experience in Judith A. Christian's elegant, simple, complex eight-word, thirteen-syllable haiku, "rising from your bed."

I have lived in two places where the sound of a train whistle could be heard late at night, a freight train passing through my nondescript town on its way from someplace wonderful (Montreal?) to someplace else wonderful (Boston? New York City?). This haiku brings me back to the lonely nights of adolescence, in my third-floor bedroom in our house on a hill above town. Not far below, the train tracks followed the Nashua River through north-central Massachusetts, a north-flowing river meandering its way to the Atlantic, a river that suffered the indignities of everything a hundred little milltowns could throw at it—and into it— before finally reaching the Merrimack and eventually the sea. Everything—train, river—going somewhere, anywhere. "Somewhere, anywhere"—the refrain of one's teen-aged years. And every night, the train whistle, which made the going sound just as forlorn as the staying. What a first word: "rising." The "I will arise, and go now" of Yeats's "The Lake Isle of Innisfree." The rising sun. A rising from the grave of one reborn, resurrected. All images of light and hope; not the stuff of this haiku. The words "darkness" and "night" are not present in these lines, and I have risen from bed in broad daylight after many an afternoon nap, but somehow we just know that this poem is set in the wee hours that offer only insomnia and longing to the one rising from bed.

Or am I wrong? Is this a poem about inspiration? The act of "remembering / the train whistle" making the poet get up immediately to write the poem about the act of "remembering / the train whistle"? And so, it could be a poem about light, after all, the light of an idea pulling into the station of one's consciousness, initiating that flurry of activity, the gathering of belongings, the disembarking, the looking around for familiar faces or landmarks. The train whistle is present in this poem, while being absent from this poem. The whistle is not heard in actual fact, but in memory. Had the actual sound reached the riser's ears five minutes earlier? Five years earlier? Fifty years and five hundred miles distant from where the bed is now located? Yes, to all of the above?

I keep coming back to this being a poem set in the dark of night. As I tell my literature students at some point each semester, I am an optimistic pessimist. Each moment, I tell them, can offer an experience of beauty to the aware observer, or to the observer who is open to the possibility of beauty. At the same time, we all know—we all know—how this journey ends. To that ending, and beyond, is where this haiku takes me each time I read it. Someone rising from bed in the middle of the night, made restless or perhaps even momentarily crazed, by the memory of something that has been lost. That something is I. This present-tense haiku is about the future, and the past. Everyone who reads this poem becomes both the rememberer and the remembered. Every barrier established by the laws of physics is meaningless, here within the world created by these eight words, by these thirteen syllables, by this gentle trickster poet.

*****

Hidden Treasure

Sometimes that tiny glint
catching your eye
is only a gum wrapper
or a pull tab.
Sometimes it's a coin,
a penny, a dime.

But, once in a great while,
it's a key.
When you dare
to pick it up,
dare to use it,
you find a secret.

Like a poem you write,
the words leading
to a quiet dim recess
where your parents
love each other
and you see it.

—Jim Berkheiser

Jim Berkheiser's poem "Hidden Treasure" not only contains but also stands as a metaphor for the haiku aesthetic. In this poem, he evokes that surface simplicity that gradually reveals deeper meaning, or rather pulls the reader in with the promise of something hidden, something worth finding. Reveal, but do not reveal too much—that is the aspect of poetic craft I see in "Hidden Treasure." It is a precarious balance, one I know I can rarely achieve with as much poise as Jim has in this poem. Exploration of that about which we are uncertain, coupled with specific information—there is another paradox of the haiku aesthetic that is present in "Hidden Treasure." I am so impressed with the images in this poem, and Jim's command of these images in the service of deeper meaning.

There are eighteen lines in this poem, yet to me it feels like a haiku: brief, yet complex in its brevity. The compact presentation of images contributes to this. The first stanza is little more than a list of shiny objects beneath our feet. "Sometimes"—so much of the balance of this poem depends on that word used twice in the first stanza, which acts as a hint that these small things are clues to some deeper mystery. In fact, look at the words the poet uses to lead us into this mysterious place: "Sometimes" in the first stanza, "but" in the second stanza, "like" in the third. Those three words hint at the story-beneath-the-story: "sometimes, but, like." The psychological resonance of metaphor is that is it a process of exploration: one is striving to make sense of an impression—make sense of a sense. Metaphors are created when we are uncertain: out of our desire to know what something *is* we describe what it is *like*. A metaphor is itself a journey towards discovery, and this poem takes us on that journey.

The power is in what those words leave out, or, rather, what they imply: Each reader will fill in his or her own missing pieces in the statement, "Sometimes _____ but like _____." The missing pieces, as in the poem, become the precious thing. The lost becomes found. This is the essence of a work of art, to return to us something we knew or perhaps didn't know we had lost. That something is usually part of our own humanity.

In his poem, Jim Berkheiser has filled in the blanks, told us the story, and yet left room for each reader to add his or her own story. He saved the metaphorical "lesson" for the end, once we were enthralled with the world of the poem in the first two stanzas. We were already beginning to superimpose our own experience onto those first two stanzas, thinking, "Yes, I've had that sometimes...sometimes...but once in a great while feeling, too...." And then that final stanza tumbles us into the metaphorical place where we all really live: the place where memory and creativity inform the way we see the world.

*****

State Street to Central, by Lark

Champagne fabulations, it may
have been stout. Tonalities,
eggs, orange juice, toast,
shades of a basket of breakfast
from Lemmie's, a brilliance of morning
held more than enough, a transport
from Jay Street in a halo of sun.
Arias rising like optical heat along
sidewalks in summer, the cool
of those courtyards, strung waving
like elegant wash, window to window,
red colorations, a spectrum of Sundays,
an Albany noon. An arc along birdstreets
from State Street to Central, by Lark.

— Chuck Tripi

Another journey, this one taking us on "an arc along birdstreets" as
we explore the impressions that arise from memory. Neuroscientists are
learning what poets have known all along: that each time a memory is
evoked, it is new—the act of remembering changes the memory. Never
the same memory twice! Chuck Tripi's "State Street to Central, by Lark"
demonstrates how this works, how we embellish memory and really cannot
exist in the present without being informed and re-informed by the past.
His poem lets us observe *how*; one aspect of the haiku aesthetic here is
that the poet leaves it up to the reader to provide an answer to *why*.

The interplay of the senses infuses this poem with imagery. From
the first two words, "Champagne fabulations," taste is stimulated, touch
(the bubbles of sparkling wine), and vision (as we picture a glass of

bubbly or the world as seen through the lifted glass), and then immediately
we are immersed in another sensory experience, "stout"—and then a
cascade of taste, texture, sights, sounds, scents, each image transforming
into the next. This poem lets us experience synesthesia. "Arias rising
like optical heat..."—sound becomes visual and vision washes over us
as warmth. And all the time we are on the move, gliding along the
streets the way we do in our dreams or in our memories, released from
the quotidian act of walking by what the poem doesn't need to spell out:
joy, love, a perfect moment of existence, happiness—this is part of
what the reader is trusted to bring to the poem.

The relationship between image and idea is a common point of
contention among those who critique and analyze poetry. "State Street
to Central, by Lark" serves as the epitome, to me, of a poem all poets
should study. In fourteen lines, images almost too numerous to count—
in fact, the poem mirrors what would happen if one were to stop right
this moment and try to "count" the sensory images one is experiencing.
Where does one image begin and the next end? Are they at all sequential,
or are they occurring simultaneously, and if so, does image plus image
equal a new image altogether? This poem is all about image the way a
painting is all about image. But it offers us some ideas, as well, from the
admission of a trick of memory in the first two lines (and what a superb
line break to underscore that trick: "it may / have been"), to a hint of the
idea of celebration in "a brilliance of morning / held more than enough,"
to the idea of relief and refuge in " the cool / of those courtyards." If
the reader could verbalize or at least intuit the ideas behind these images,
the poem and the things in the poem would be meaningless. The poem
is all about meaning the way a painting is all about meaning.

The meaning may be, in fact, the search for meaning, that existential
journey from which we never truly rest. They are breath-taking, Judith
Christian's "rising from your bed," Jim Berkheiser's "Hidden Treasure,"
and Chuck Tripi's "State Street to Central, by Lark." Imagery, motion,

mystery, memory, and enough left unsaid for the reader to add a body of personal experience. Each poem is complete unto itself, yet is also a starting point from which the reader is compelled to leap into a familiar, newly-discovered world.

*****

The delight, when reading a poem, of recognizing what one realizes one has known all along. The surprising ways one moment informs the following moment; *non sequitur* made logical by the poet's suggestion and the reader's acceptance of the connection(s) between moments. Image as a vehicle for meaning, image as the cart to meaning's horse. Precision of language, psychological authenticity of line breaks, a delight in paradox, and other elements of poetic craft enhanced (where necessary and where possible) by a willingness to revise. All these are contained in the term "the haiku aesthetic." All are essential for any poem, not just for haiku and related short-forms.

I have not included a discussion of the "rules" or even definitions of haiku, tanka, of haibun. A quick internet search of these poetic forms can be a fascinating exercise in contradiction. I do not avoid this topic when I give a haiku workshop, but my "instruction" comes down to this: Rules are guidelines. It is more informative and more creative and more inspiring to read a variety of haiku, tanka, and haibun by a variety of authors. Learn the "rules" as a way to—I won't say as a way to "break" them, but as a way to make the rules your own. Come to an understanding of what the haiku aesthetic means by observing how poets put it into practice in their own work. Then, make the haiku aesthetic your own, as well. Find your own ways of answering the question, "Is it a good poem," whether your poem be three lines or thirty.

is it a good poem—
all these orange lilies
lining every road

About the Author

Jean LeBlanc teaches writing and literature at Sussex County Community College in Newton, New Jersey, U.S.A. Her poetry has appeared in numerous journals, including the *Lullwater Review*, *Bellevue Literary Review*, *Journal of New Jersey Poets*, *Kerf*, *Modern Haiku*, *Frogpond* (the journal of the Haiku Society of America), *Ribbons* (the journal of the Tanka Society of America), and *Modern English Tanka*. She is the executive editor of the Paulinskill Poetry Project in Andover, New Jersey, and editor of their anthology *Voices From Here* (2009). She does editorial work for Cyberwit.net, including editing the anthology *A World Rediscovered* (2012). Her books are *Just Passing Through: Tanka, Haiku, Haibun* (Paulinskill Poetry Project, 2007), *The Stream Singing Your Name: Tanka and Sijo* (Modern English Tanka Press, 2009), *Where We Go: Haiku and Tanka Sequences and Other Concise Imaginings* (Modern English Tanka Press, 2010), and *At Any Moment* (Backwaters Press, 2010). More of her work can be seen on her website, <www.jeanleblancpoetry.com>.